D0833870

Country

Also by D. H. Melhem

Poetry

Notes on 94th Street
Rest in Love
Children of the House Afire
Mosaic: Poems from an IWWG Workshop (editor)

Prose

Blight: A Novel
Heroism in the New Black Poetry
Gwendolyn Brooks: Poetry and the Heroic Voice
Reaching Exercises: The IWWG Workshop Book

Musical Drama

Children of the House Afire

For Issa J. Boullata —
With warm admiration and highest esteem
D.H. Melhem
January 5, 2001

Country

AN ORGANIC POEM

D.H. MELHEM

Cross-Cultural Communications
Merrick, New York
1998

Copyright © 1998 by D. H. Melhem

All rights reserved. No part of this book may be reproduced, in any form, without permission from the publisher or author, unless by a reviewer who wishes to quote brief passages.

Acknowledgments

Sections 11, 18, and 53 of "country" first appeared in *Confrontation.* Sections 29 and 36 were published together as "Reflecting Waters" in *Home Planet News.* Section 49 begins the introduction to my *Heroism in the New Black Poetry* (University Press of Kentucky, 1990). *The East Hampton Star* printed an earlier version of Section 51. Parts of "Cross-Country Journal" first appeared as follows: "Visit" in *Oxalis,* "West Glacier" in *Pivot,* "At Livonia" and "Mac" in *The New Press.* To all, grateful acknowledgment is made.

Grateful acknowledgment is also accorded to the New York State Council on the Arts and the National Endowment for the Arts whose past seed grants, in part, have made this publication possible.

This project was brought to life by the faithful dedication of my publisher and fellow poet, Stanley H. Barkan.

Published in the United States by
Cross-Cultural Communications
239 Wynsum Avenue
Merrick, NY 11566-4725
Tel: (516) 868-5635
Fax: (516) 379-1901

First Edition, 1998

Library of Congress Cataloging-in-Publication Data

Melhem, D. H.
Country : an organic poem / D. H. Melhem.
p. cm.
ISBN 0-89304-222-6 (hard cover : alk. paper). —
ISBN 0-89304-223-4 (pbk. : alk. paper)
I. Title.
PS3563.E442C68 1998
811'.54—dc21   97-24177
                                            CIP

Book design by the Mya Kramer Design Group
Printed in the United States of America

for my Mother and Father, their immigrant dreams

———•———

for Chester, Dana, Gregory, George, and Tess, fulfilling

———•———

to the memory of Margaret W. Cook, mentor, friend

———•———

and to the memory of

Ree Dragonette, Percy E. Johnston, Barbara A. Holland

a splendor of voices

CONTENTS

CALIFORNIA SUITE

INDIANA FARM SUITE

*The earth also was corrupt before God, and the earth was
filled with violence.*

— GENESIS 6.11

—◆—

*The history of our country the past hundred years has
been a series of assumptions and usurpations of power
over women, in direct opposition to the principles of just
government, acknowledged by the United States as its
foundation . . . for the violation of these fundamental
principles of our government, we arraign our rulers on
this Fourth day of July, 1876.*

— *Declaration of Rights for Women*

—◆—

*Confess that to severe eyes, using the moral microscope
upon humanity, a sort of dry and flat Sahara appears . . .
pervading flippancy and vulgarity, low cunning,
infidelity—everywhere an abnormal libidinousness,
unhealthy forms. . . .*

— WALT WHITMAN, *Democratic Vistas,* 1871

I. COUNTRY

*I am sure what I said is true,— namely, that
history, at bottom is an account of the efforts . . .
to find freedom and show love.*

— JAMES JACKSON PUTNAM

Preface for Ralph Waldo Emerson

Free as a spark
from a roman candle
a leaf snapped
by a wind amassing
its persistent powers
I, temporary and severe
in the solitary rigor of a dance
am caught up into spectacle

the eye is the first circle
from me to you, shaping
within a universal motion
our permanent possibilities

Preface for Walt Whitman

One's-self I sing, a simple separate person,
Yet utter the word Democratic, the word En-Masse.

Poem of my life
from you I extrapolate a country
as your particles assemble and cohere
on my palette of rainbow mountains
that range a geography of waste images
to compose
a simple, separate person
who has dreamed America
a long, hard time . . .

1.

I sing the generous dead who live with me
companionate their silence fills the still page
of my day

body is deficient   loud   metamorphic
cannot be long held

yet I praise toward our speechless act
conversations : printed

2.

George Washington: :
you have addressed me
in the resonance of your portrait
the marble statue your conscience
a vein in stone pulses
the temple your brain
columns that span rivers

Catalogue 122 : : AMERICANA with an emphasis on
California and the West. Bookmarket, Hollywood, CA.

An Eulogy on the Illustrious Life and Character of George Washington. 21 pp. Sewn.

An Oration on the Sublime Virtues of General George Washington. Disbound.

Thoughts on the Cause of the Present Discontents. In excellent condition.

3.

iconic earth
slave to production
shifts my white into
ocher   umber
marks me deciduous
evergreen   lumber

Philadelphia
a quill from hand to hand
makes a circle
of imagination
whose outer rings
whirl into constellations
galactic encounters

the universe expands
contracts
and plantain firms its position
in bypassed roadbeds

A Review of the Policy of the United States Government Which Led to the War of 1812. Cloth, scuffed, faded and stained.

Benjamin Franklin's Morals of Chess. Front outer hinge cracked about 2 inches.

Lectures on School-Keeping. In a 1/2 morocco folding slipcase. A good tight copy.

Inquiry into the Object and Tendency of the Present War. Oracle Press. Unopened. Manuscript corrections.

The Stranger in America. Signed by the author.

4.

Buttes risen from the sea
Colorado
and this is the fourfold river of hell
Colorado
and I am chastened by currents
of terror and violence

But my mind lives in the rectitude
of visions
that fly through the raised eyes of Thoreau
from the bottom of the Grand Canyon—
that burning lake of angels who have drowned
and rise again, level after level of shale, rock, and stubble,
the brown face of Thoreau implanted like his garden
of simple connections to the whole surface of life :

From the shade of his hands issues the evergreen soul
of John Brown, sheltered also by Harriet Tubman and Milton,
Shelley and Kant, Susan B. Anthony and W. E. B. Du Bois
who visit in resolute clouds of sunlight and water
where Emerson is singing the words he has lost
and Whitman makes them new

They watch over this Canyon with the dead
who howl their packed remembrances
across twenty-eight miles
the red dust of a tarnished land

History of the Captivity and Sufferings of Maria Martin Who was Six Years a Slave in Algiers. Rebound into modern cloth. Paper heavily browned.

A View of the Conduct of the Executive, in the Foreign Affairs of the United States. An uncut copy. Rare in this state.

A Report of a Committee of the Humane Society. Unopened and uncut.

A Sketch of the Life and Services of John Quincy Adams. Disbound.

White Conquest. Shelfworn.

Massasoit of the Wampanoags. Privately printed.

Indians of the United States. The American Museum of Natural History.

5.

Because you are waves massed to the height of their breaking
I can see you from this Canyon in my tallest perceptions
across the swift current of my shadow
the bright angel shale ascended from a brown and red rippling
rain smiting rocks downward to the riverbanks
and snow lifted in pine branches
to redemptive weather

I, Henry Thoreau   displaced from a burning coast
my grave rocking with high falls
John Brown hanged   my garden turned under
with my accounts of transvalue
and how the earth might become
changed

I am changed   removed to the dangling
                                of a stiffnecked madman
dead Indians and slaves
who color the Canyon

Jefferson Davis, Ex-President of the Confederate States of America, A Memoir. Front hinges (inners) are cracked.

Brown America: The Story of a New Race. The Friendship Press.

The Underground Rail Road. A Record of Facts, Authentic Narratives, Letters &c., Narrating the Hardships, Hair-breadth Escapes, and Death Struggles of the Slaves in their Efforts for Freedom, as related by Themselves and Others, or Witnessed by the Author. Portraits from Photographs from Life.

Landlord and Tenant on the Cotton Plantation. Works Progress Administration.

Sixty Years of California Song. Good copy.

6.

Wounded Knee
barters the bullets
of my ancestry

my arm the arrow
bent gesture of a dead sun
hanging among clouds
under the broken moon
ghostflowers rise

I am a victim of
precision
that seizes
my proud ages
trout in its water
the deer meadow
driven into
history

blood   my black hair
bind the story

remembered sun
raising your living face to us
speak radiance

Memoir of the Life and Public Services of John Charles Fremont, including an Account of his Explorations, Discoveries and Adventures on Five Successive Expeditions across the North American Continent. Cloth, faded and dustsoiled. Inner front hinge, cracked.

War Poems 1898. Scarce.

Gold is the Cornerstone. With vignettes.

The Missions and Missionaries of California. Volume I. Foldout maps.

The Missions and Missionaries of California. Volume II. Foldout maps.

Angel City in Turmoil. Fine copy.

Address on the Peculiar Advantages of the United States in Comparison with Other Nations. Disbound. Minor foxing.

Buccaneers Gold. Fine copy.

Buccaneers Gold. Another copy. Slightly worn.

Iniciativa sobre el fondo piadoso de Californias. Three statements concerning the pious funds from the California missions. Mexican broadside.

The Mediterranean Shores of America. Small chip at back hinge, slightly chipped around edges.

7.

fingers of the horseman:
        bit or bradoon
        caveson   browband
        show bridle   snaffle
            (listen, o horse, and run

his feet:
        stirrup and girth
        and the super never rust spurs
        hunt spur and show spur

as naturalist:
        hay rack   tack box
        breeding hopple
            (listen, o horse, and run

hands of the horseman:
        riding crop   training whip
        driving whip
        lunge whip
        fly whisk
        jockey bat
            (listen, o horse, and run

run   bolt   jump
climb   shake   butt
run, o horse, from the leather eyes
of the rider

8.

At the O.T.B. window your ticket
marked with the time and three letters
because you must try to get out of
the place you are posted
because your ticket is white
green and yellow
like a new season
with brown horses
a pretty ticket
numbers
of solitary dreaming
because gamblers dream
for themselves and imagine
at the end they include you
gamblers the bettors the dreamers
the horse junkies
of two-dollar windows
that close them out
every evening

In the last race
a ringer

The Investigators
bear
investigating

Under the saddle of foolish hopes
one recorded as a dead horse
whose insurance was collected
by the owner who ran him
for a half-dead nag
whom he looked like
paid fifty-seven
to one

If chance were
a true variable
and the track the weather
the weltering
were all
then you'd be merely
misguided

In the saddle
wearing a peaked cap
Venality rides
light as a last breath
swift as a spark
wins the wager
pennies in the torn pocket
wins the new boots
the bit
the crop and the bridle

That rider borrows
your eyes O lost love
squinting myopic
quick from your pocket
trades the dream of we
for the dream of me
runs a horse
discharging power
belonging
to the life
you run

9.

You did not buy the running shoes
you planned to run in
you planned
to stop smoking and prepare
to run in your new running shoes
which you did not buy
though you planned to run
in them   you wanted to stop
gambling and smoking to start
running again in your
running shoes   you did not
buy the equipment
you were waiting
for impulse

10.

A life lived over your shoulder
dislocated   you say
by care   unraveling into
ropes   into whips and scourges
you range the cleft of chaos
hired to beat back time
to assassinate ideas
of Divine order
of community
hired to expatriate
the God of Love
downtown
into your sequined shoes and a cigar
pimp dandy with a fancy cane

Your brother your employer
wears hand-tailored three-piece pin-striped suits
and the finest English leather boots with spurs
dug into the haunches of a chauffeur
pulling   through ticker-tape quotations
an antique chariot
custom-built abroad
filled with stocks and bondage

Your brother-employer
buys you
a Cadillac large enough
for the harlot sisters industrial
to ride in

11.

Baths of a Continent !
You would have to be
invented: damp, dim, and cold, and hot,
like Hell, the state where people entertain
by trial; those who are enclosed
in circular argument, in copulative
selves, their chattering teeth, the puffs of steam
that follow them upstairs, from pool to
table for massage, et cetera,
from benches where they sit in their white towels,
chat and judge the singers. As water runs into the pool
and floors are mechanically polished by whistling bristles,
the auditioners and their piano and guitars and drum
sing their experience and inexperience,
the few excellent voices shimmering above
the diffusions. The raw boy, unmarinated,
so to speak, and warbling "God Bless the Child,"
is hired on the spot, "for the trade."

The steam, the soap, and the water
do not purify. For all the scrubbing
and bathing, nothing gets clean
where life is commercial, when it floats
unguented with art, and the price
of young boys or young daughters
is set in a market, with microphones
to inspire the bidding.

The Tendency of History. Reprint.

History of the United States of America. The Author's Last Revision. Elaborately gilt spine, over marbled boards. Marbled endpapers.

Kentucky, Tennessee & Ohio Almanack, for the Year of Our Lord 1804. Stabbed. Edges frayed, stained along upper margin throughout.

The Church in America. Good copy.

Ideas for a Science of Good Government. Rubbed.

A Plain and Serious Address to the Master of a Family on the Important Subject of Family Religion. Last leaf blank. Stabbed.

Outline of a Course of Astronomical Lectures by Joseph Emerson, whose interest in female education was aroused by the writings of Hannah More. Opened a seminary for young women in 1816, distinguished by the range of subjects offered—subjects at that time which were not considered suitable for young women. $22.50.

12.

Blown to the silo top
chopped cornstalks husks and ears
pile up, ferment
their tasty succulence
green feed in winter.

Farmers transport to granary
wheat, barley, and corn
to store for transshipment
dry grain, hire
a gondola car from the railroad
to market in Omaha Minneapolis
Milwaukee Wichita St. Louis—
major grain buyers.

Ensilage ferments
its tasty succulence
to livestock.

13.

I sought the last whispers of just men and women
that could infuse this bawd corpse
its maquillage of new steel
I walked the Great Plains
where no growing seed was obstruction
to see (like Whitman, like Emerson)
into the impulse of things

Rugged through Indiana I hiked and over Ohio
through the drift deposit of calcareous loam
toward brown-splattered clouds of milch cows
bulls and barbed-wire fences
daisies waiting in the prairie of their day
as I wait in the permanence of my ordinary heartbeat

Considerations on the Currency and Banking System of the United States. Modern plain brown wrappers, stabbed, slightly frayed, light to moderate foxing.

Progress and Poverty: An Inquiry into the Cause of Industrial Depressions, and of Increase of Want with Increase of Wealth—the Remedy. Spine, faded and chipped.

The Missing Chapter in the Life of Abraham Lincoln. Fine copy.

I Saw Booth Shoot Lincoln. $12.50.

America on Stone.

The Marvel of Nations. Our Country: Its Past, Present, and Future, and What the Scriptures Say of It. Battle Creek.

The West Point Atlas of American Wars. Fine copies.

Narrative of the Massacre at Chicago. Rebound into full brown morocco with gilt lettering. A fine copy.

A Guide for Emigrants. A little scuffed at edges.

Report of the Committee on Public Lands. 4 pages.

street of crazies
whose despair thickens
the white paving
and stomps the gutters
like buffalo returning
as energy

I imagine you with mothers and fathers
the street become daisies
where you run
your cloven childhood
shedding into praise   and dancing

The City of the Saints. Head and foot of spine show wear.

Rivers of America.

Animal Life of Yellowstone Park. 2 photos of author laid in front.

Border Fights & Fighters. Decorative cloth.

Charles W. Quantrell: A True History of His Guerrilla Warfare on the Missouri and Kansas Border during the Civil War of 1861 to 1865. Illustrated.

The Expeditions of Zebulon Montgomery Pike. 6 folded maps.

Military Life in Dakota. Indexed.

Buffalo Land: An Authentic Account of the Discoveries, Adventures, and Mishaps of a Scientific and Sporting Party in the Wild West; Replete with Information, Wit and Humor. The Appendix comprising a complete Guide for Sportsmen and Emigrants. Outer hinges beginning to crack. Corners, worn.

15.

California unachieved
the place intended
prospect
the way
flared briefly
private ore
magic

16.

to write the country
as a poem
incomplete
is the truth
of geography

17.

House on Sunset Boulevard
hanging among magnolias
over lawns   floating

red tile roof and white columns
curve toward a golden past
in fluid composure

dream your blue green
dream silver

18.

Coney Island

Over the Bridge and East River
my eyes Hart Crane and the Brooklyn span
I take the steel road to Sea Beach
the past rolling through wheels
of the N train whose new cars
speak no and never
to old vehicles junkyarded
in memory

Beholding the Stillwell Avenue Station
from elevated tracks
I descend the desolate ramp
jostled by ghost-crowds
their bathing bags and picnic lunches
their smell of coffee and expectations
they walk they walk with me
my hand in my mother's
to see Coney Island
to ride the Ferris Wheel
eat at Nathan's

We will swim in the ocean
thrashing a small space
for ourselves

But
having taken the N train
I go down the ramp alone
my hand extended to you O Sorrow

to you O happy invention
and there through the gates
at the foot of incline
on the streets of ice cream
the way of delight
is closed   the Tornado
is closed   I run to the Boardwalk—
door to a childhood of 31 Rides
Steeplechase The Funny Place
boarded up   Kiddie Ride
churns empty cars
toward the sea
pinched by jetties

I step down to the salt edge
with birdcries dredged from clearing water

What is retrieved ?

Gulls paddling like ducks
in a pool hewn by rain
clouds opening a fan
across the sun
clouds bunching like sheep
to the right
arrows to the left

What is retrieved ?

Reader/Adviser Speaks
Seven Languages   Babel tongues
the starry stripes
flap with the flag
of the Polar Bear Club

Yearlong bathers
share winter sun
on a concrete slab

A tough leans over
the Boardwalk railing
aims at naked feet
and spits

I walk on
to the subway
chilled

19.

. . . yet doth he devise means that his banished be not expelled from him.

— 2 SAMUEL 14:14

God loves me   in a rudimentary way
dips my head into the sea   anchors my body
in a garden
burns my lips with thirst
bears me on a current of wild air
to be dropped
into the wormy-armed puddle
where I sink and swim

God loves me   I think
I am told this
in a cup of spring water
under a goshawk sky

20.

Culture is not the self, not a confection
gobbled anonymous at
a cotton candy seashore

On the boardwalk I paint you in the contours
of your colors
Write me a poem as I render your image
tell me yourself, our tangents and integrations

with reverent ear let us listen into a shell
for breakers   and the dangerous sun

21.

Induction run motors that transfer power directly to the blade. See the saw the quiet saw for $30 LESS than in our Spring Big Book. Disposable framing blades, coarse-tooth, not craftsman. For fast, rip cuts. Dadoes: not for radial saws with universal motors. Cut fine veneers and other sensitive materials with little or no splintering. (See *skin.*) Save 50% on this drill. Speed. Control. Speed control. Replacement parts. (See *limbs.*) You may need new Shocks. We have it!

  abdominal supports
  abrasive belts
  BABY GOODS
  ethnic styles!

An outstanding value model 200 pump-action shotgun. Only $139.95. Slug gun. Semi-automatic shotgun. Only. Standard model 300. Only. Over-and-under lets you fire without switching triggers. Only. Single-shot double-barrel bolt-action muzzle-loading auto-load high-powered lever-action made for us. Only. Power zoom scopes. Round-view lenses. Compound hunting bows. Take-down hunting bow. Siliconized deep-pile acetate lining gun case to protect from moisture damage. A great idea. Only. Monogramming decal kit included. True center shot. We have it! See

  clocks cleaners darkroom supplies fences fireplaces
  flame resistants furnaces grooming supplies guards
  guitar lessons gun ammunition life insurance
  mastectomy bras mowers mufflers Christmas tree
  ornaments nursery stock pool accessories quilts
  fishing rods roots workclothes, etc.

Where America Shops

INDEX
>dress suits
>jump suits
>abdominal supports
>abrasive discs
>adapters
>adhesives

the things that are for sale
BAGS
>accessory
>cargo
>food
>garment
>shoe
>sportmen's
>tote
>trash
>traveling

the things that are for sale
>cabinets, canoes, gasoline-powered Hole Diggers
>portable heaters with solid-state ignition

COLORMATES in thick plush pile—
>"When a colored surface is fixated,
>it soon begins to look pale" (R. Arnheim)

I keep looking at you—less black, and I—less white? looking at
each other—seeing more and less—we keep looking . . .

22.

Walt Whitman
I think of poets
who invoke you like
some compendious vagrom
and how you encompass
even the frailty
of their poems

23.

O Ezra Pound! Usura usura
you wail in the wilderness of factual data
that retrieves a vestigial tradition
in defiance of dawn communicating
to botched generations of men and women
crying their suffering unheard
as they run uphill
among Blakean mountains

24.

a pass a down a field goal
kicking a ball the taut skin of a pig
with blunt toes on cowhide
helmeted heads the shoulders padded gargantuan
to hit em again harder harder harder

offensive teams defensive teams
tackle and run at strangers trained
to run against them   rituals of battle
rituals of riot   pain deployed into clocks
sixty minutes   iron cheers

25.

never going to be innocent together walking toward that day
where the river lifts the sky   never going to be sun or moon or
rainbow or branch of glowing juniper   never going to be the
things we dream for each other or give unfamiliar streets our
stride   never going to make us into time   except the grave
unloving tale without words   hacked torso of hope   dumped

26.

(to the tune of "My Devotion")

My devotion
is endless and deep as a notion

This sensation
is ending depressed as the nation

27.

sky without stars without hope without help
listlessly drifting to dawn and day
scatter your nebulous shards
like seeds to my lips

28.

bright world in morning light
touch these blind scrawls to write
the dawn still young in me
inscribe my tongue

to ocean   rain to come
rice in the sky   wheat from the sun

like pine cones on a raging forest floor
heart   heart   break open

29.

ocean   you roll your days
telling me it's o.k.
that everything will happen anyway
and you will survive events and gradual weather
but I figure in a human dimension of quick rhythms
of which you   are the farthest delineation

swimming in my own time I can hear
the swimmers about me
some surrendering   floating   into deep water
others at the edge of the blows   never enter

we who have learned your ineluctable ways
dive into waves that come too fast or too high

30.

I am Odysseus and this ship, self, ocean, landfall
in the wind of time's eye reddened with your blood,
brother, sister, friend—O Father! you have waited for me.
Mother: I have seen your shade upon my steps; you whisper—
from what shore?—would have me fling this spirit-web,
its spume of stars, into the wake of my wave-deep passage.
With rudder but no anchor, no hawser-line,
an eye only to look ahead with memory
discerns the One Life that lives on
bow to stern, and warms
my hand upon this wheel.

31.

line and color :
    diagonal force moves into the plane
                  and can rise

Black woman   :   your visual fingers
draw earth over this canvas
in need of ground for ideas to grow
from natural plans that life has to continue

the horsechestnut blooms the hand of Harriet Tubman
the sparrow's eye on the dawn line
is Sojourner Truth

32.

The underlying sense of form in my work has been the system of the Universe, or part thereof. For that is a rather large model to work from.

— ALEXANDER CALDER

maps   contiguous
surprise   at contact
is it you and I traveling   who make
connections?   heartbeat and dusty-shoed
conversations   in the wind   suppose
I ranged through centuries
toward Spartacus
Jesus leading the troops of the poor
loving thoughts on papyrus
would my essential ore
press into coal
fuel fire
at the dense core
of fathering mothering issues?

you and I   tangential
bring fragmentary messages
from stars   there are
connections   we learn
to become them   slowly   not without
effort

33.

Eleanor Roosevelt
            walking underground to workers
reminds a president that what he can't see
exists

I saw you once in my high school auditorium
thought you were not real   having stepped out of
the radio and *The New York Times*
you had a kind voice that spoke to loneliness

you were
beautiful

34.

A knowledge of subsurface structure in advance of drilling has resulted in the discovery of production at depths previously considered impossible.

— "Petroleum," s.v., *Encyclopedia Britannica*

Regarding petroleum, its reservoir rocks, a knowledge of subsurface structure in advance of drilling is essential. Knowledge has resulted in the discovery of oil at unexpected depths; those previously considered impossible. Based upon geological data, new pools have been found. The matter is stratigraphic, not structural, to find what we find at certain levels, to go deeper and take more, to take more from depleted wells, to inject the rock with acid and take more, to penetrate and loosen, to make straighter holes in the earth and protect the equipment. As pools are exhausted, as prospecting techniques are exhausted, others arrive in time. They progress to exhaustion, exhaustion is progress, as the pools are depleted, progress produces, and others arrive in time.

35.

the sun is
behind you
as you go to dawn
a map of stars
in your pocket
a timetable
of constellations
you travel by

Griffin, Georgia
stars
fill the eyes of the heifer
turn sandhills crystalline
lift wings upon horses
light human faces
many stars
to conjure by

your mother waits
holding stars
in her apron
your father hoes
the starry earth
his back is sore
his feet merge
with the soil of his workshoes
he awaits you
and the map of stars
that is country
a blue pavement of cities
birth brightness
and you
free of the plough
and the poverty
on a visit

36.

a poverty: not to receive or give
what can secure the day's intrinsic stars
the hand in hand the brow uplifted
and the unburdening of death

not to receive or give
is futureless   ad hoc
nothing until performance acts
upon event and actor and the necessary
chance the computations of a marketplace

world's a weary wisdom   has two heads
                                                    one mirroring
a gargoyle on a burning lake
of desperate energies
the other   rattles its dry seedpods
of anticipation and blunt endeavor
toward a humane universe

37.

Person   place   thing   tree
each in its living space

I learned from my grandmother
to save the string that ties
the past into epiphany
and sets it down to die by fire

On the sixth of January
one returns to a new year—
familiar rooms that house
a self unwieldy
strung with parcels
the sacks and suitcases
of tarnished ornaments
a self   difficult to manage
with grace   stumbling fallible myopic
retaining the once-dazzled vision
as a portable lost occasion

38.

Stars, like human beings, tend to be gregarious. In the immediate vicinity of the sun out to a distance of 5 parsecs or about 16 light-years, we have been able to detect 31 single stars, 9 binaries, and 2 triple systems. Thus of the 55 stars considered in this nearby volume of space, almost half are members of complex families. Although we do not have as precise a census of stars at greater distances, our data tend to confirm the conclusion that about half of the stars in our own Milky Way are members of complex or multiple systems.

— DONALD H. MENZEL, *Astronomy*

I am calling you   Albert Einstein   your
parallels melding in suns round their strong matters
mixing significance
                bed so sweet
                bed so sweet
you are my Albert Einstein   I feel close to your
intelligence   we relate   several ancient equations
                          bed so sweet

it will never be again   I deny you and
love you   betrayer of my
euclidean circles   this clock   this clattering of
eyeblink   bozoclown dickering with eternity

you lie in your false teeth your illfitting choppers that
clack clack   your wellsitting buckets that drip
as the crow flies

let one live and die truly
a slab of dead fact   elegy compost
to celebration, perhaps   mourn truly
I mourn   it will never be again   you return as a textbook
another person   laughing behind mirrors of recollections

I am calling you   Albert Einstein

39.

We are cast down
before desolate altars
and broken images
the dead carcasses of children
scattered about

Make a chain:
for the land is full of bloody crimes,
and the city is full of violence

— *see* Ezekiel 6, 7

Your foster father signed you up. Farmboy, you smoked grass, banked the ashes of a war.

A cop now, in plainclothes, you take the muggers as the pimps move off. The corner supermarket guard looks at you over sale rice in the window. A drunk vomits against a new Buick sedan. Five black pickets and one white carry their homemade signs outside the store, protest the firing of a black cashier with eight years' service to the grocer raising the hardest prices on Broadway, who canned her and the clerk who got past her with corned beef hash.

You watch for an inward signal that something better may rise at the corner, you thinking of grass, a high memorial grass to lie in, to hide you and a theoretical enemy you practiced, grass huts afire with rice to be burned, grass crying its hidden throats into smoke, to smoke your heart tranquil again as the distant green blades of your child's day.

40.

Last night we rode into the Bronx
your cop's badge on the floor of your Firebird
gold goblet filled with California chablis
you at the wheel over Bruckner Boulevard
and the South Bronx tottering tottering
empty figures of reflected light
and you said, yes, this is a really gold goblet
I thought I deserved something at last
and you sipped from the gold so gracefully
and spoke of the house you would buy
with two jobs and your young life

Drive into the Bronx for a smoke
into furtive night with five dollars
the kid slinking up with a bag
after the police car cruises by and you ask me,
are you wearing a bra?
and you give me the packet to hide there
we ride up to Gun Hill Manor
behind Roman statuary
where you roll the little paper
and light it
I accept from your lips
what I do not want
but the sharing
is my heart's value

Drive into sacred adventure
like the time you went to Virginia
to dig in the night for buried treasure
and reclaim your foster father's land

The Bronx
burned
its buildings lean and groan
into smoke, rubble, and darkness
nobody lives here nobody loves these ghost buildings
the land has been lost
there has been a great wickedness
even the fires
go out

How cool you are
the way you love me
piecemeal   airborne
extending the cup

41.

Education is out there,

in the street, man—

I told you of the Beast, and Beauty, and that the Beast was how
he saw himself, and was treated, although the handsome Prince
within his skin was the virtue of his soul, and how Beauty
approached with a single candle flickering away the dark to
disclose the perfection of his blackness, and the drops of white
tallow that burned him awake to his death by a stream where
Beauty followed, and her tears upon him as she cried, "Ma
Bête!" And beneath those tears the loving Prince of his desire
rose to embrace her as they were received by the stream that
grew everywhere into its pervasive tributaries, nourishing the
dessicated land. And I wept, that the joyful Prince could not
speak in you, that you feared and raged along the banks of
your spirit, that you could feel upon your skin, as yet,
only the tallow . . .

42.

jeans cut at the crotch
jacket back studded S*U*I*C*I*D*E
    they cross the bar   vanish
    with a man banishing
    perplexity
        into folds of his rock star cape

that explodes
christ satan gloves balloons tigers tricks
whipchains   billboards   a road
        a pond with twelve ducks
the smell of ducks   lottery tickets   garbage

43.

pimp
did anyone love you little
or hate you then?
is commission
your contact?
are power and poverty
so mixed in you
that the girl
you subdue
who trusts you
to protect
her small interest
is your pride
the tarnished iridescence
of a hatband?

did Adam Smith, Vanderbilt, Morgan
or Rockefeller
weave your pallet of prurience?
did they teach you the fun of the profit
the enterprise?
entrepreneur, landlord without land
sultan of slumbodies
you parade their gargoyle emblem
for a pair of new shoes
in a passing style
for a roll with butter
for a tinkling trinket
and a dream-puffing weed

boss, now
selling your sister

44.

meanwhile at the capital
horses gallop off carrousels
ridden by children who have just read
the Declaration of Independence
and are speeding to Constitution Avenue

the TPF
            fill helmets with candy
            and cycle beside tanks that are tired

            we free you
            from prisons of your misconceptions
the children cry
waving their fine nets
to catch lies

their horses sing

45.

    he's coming   a jackass   riding high signs
        in stirrups of slogans
          animal curried
              by dirty minds
                      a jackass

46.

Special to The Times

A rock-like substance, discovered in the topsoil of North Dakota, emits fragmentary conversation upon contact. Surgical teams in Nome, Alaska, St. Petersburg, Florida, and Brooklyn, New York, have removed similar matter with verbal properties from the brains of newborn infants. The theory has been proposed that some displaced medium of infinity is retrieving audiotape erasures, and that the spotty memorial process will continue.

47.

crude oil
speeches
piped
through channels
of tv

48.

through gates of water
flushed executives corrupt all shores with
cabinets of disease-bearing organisms
radioactive CIA
carcinogenic hypocrisy
casting mutagenic smiles upon dead fish
putrid green algae among oil slicks
of american dollars

49.

Prospectus

Listen to the Winds, O God the Reader, that wail across the whip-cords stretched taut on broken human hearts; listen to the Bones, the bare bleached bones of slaves, that line the lanes of Seven Seas and beat eternal tom-toms in the forests of the laboring deep; listen to the Blood, the cold thick blood that spills its filth across the fields and flowers of the Free; listen to the Souls that Wing and thrill and weep and scream and sob and sing above it all. What shall these things mean, O God the Reader? You know. You know.

— W. E. B. Du Bois

A new poetry, strong and true, has been developing in this country. Energized by the constant quest in the Black community for emancipation and leadership, this poetry shares idealistic strains with the dominant culture and expresses the democratic intentions of American civilization. In response to decadence and isolation, it offers vigor and commonality, a cohesiveness both spiritual and heroic. The poets themselves, often describing the literature as "revolutionary," essentially view it as a politicized spiritual force. . . .

50.

country of my copybook
a colored flag   gaffhooked
the battered sky
rocks   birds   blood
    a tidal spray   shimmering
        anticipations
               that vanish

eyeless
against ocean pillars
whose vengeance drowns ?

tears will not chasten our time
revive its sorrowful bones

serpents glisten serene
having feasted on failure
its entrails drawn over
the terrible altars of history
       take   eat
       this was a body given

even bread is taken away
you will claw your coffinboards—
I am alive   I am inside   myself

death
unselective   receives
        every wing having nested
        every mate extended
        every labor in its useful skin
        descended like kings
        like one life
        that cannot forgive itself
        that pulls down the shades of its shame

51.

On the ferry to Bedloe's Island, my mother holding my hand,
the excursion seems like a visit to a lonely friend. You are a
reader, too, clutching your book (any poems in it?). And you are
kind, letting us prowl about your insides, sheltering us with your
robes. We pulse through the arteries of your circular metal
stairs. Who but my mother could be so accepting? You look a
little like her, I think, as she tells me how she cherished your
image during those days on Ellis Island, waiting with her family
to be admitted to this country.

You need us. You take us in for the company and trust us to say
your meaning. We need you to give it form: metal of collective
memory, ore that speaks, light that lives.

52.

Fourth of July: On the Hudson

barge-riding gods of fireworks
shoot color into stars stars and a firmament
light breaking over nightwater
over oilslick and striped bass
embankments of children eyebright amazed
their elders assembled smiling   rich also
in the generous hues of their garments and faces
raising salutes and sparklers and candles
that burst into the booming center
the riverspace north and south
a joining rejoicing a healing
of peace for these people
poor no more and without rancor embracing

a celebration

53.

Man walks to the river, shouldering
a long pole. Fishing rod?

A sewage dump, you say. But I cling
here, skin against glass, window of my sight
my soul leaping like a hooked trout upstream,
gills opening their pale dawn.
I can catch the sun in my mouth that sings
ribbons of light to you.
I remember the brisk river
I rode as a child
into the salt wedge of my spirit that,
wild and silvering, touched roofs,
went whooping into the air.

Look at her! Look at her!
my space thought. She is one of us—
she is none of us. She is
herself, as we are,
particles of now.

54.

And still the dream leans over parapet
toward a river of elusive fish,
the blue-hatted woman with a book,
dogs ambling grassward in sunlight.
Mind comes to rest in its images,
enjoying them one by one from a vista
over apple tree with apples
above reach, by a plane tree
turning wild. Wilderness crouches
on high branches, in thickets, glides
at evening along riverbank, grows inward.
On a summer Sunday I leave the scene, enter
the air-conditioned supermarket, buy
an onion, apples, bread, and canned sardines.

55.

Each of the walls is 246.75' long. They meet at an angle of 125°, 12', pointing exactly to the northeast corners of the Washington Monument and Lincoln Memorial. The walls are supported along their entire length by 140 concrete pilings driven approximately 35 feet to bedrock. At their vertex the walls are 10.1' in height. The stone for the walls, safety curbs and walkways is black granite quarried near Bangalore, India. All cutting and fabrication was done in Barre, Vermont. . . .

The names and inscriptions were gritblasted in Memphis, Tennessee. . . . The names were arranged chronologically and typeset in Atlanta, Georgia, from a computer tape of the official Vietnam casualty list. The letters are .53" high, and approximately .038" deep. A total of 58,209 names are inscribed on the walls.

— Vietnam Veterans Memorial brochure

Raising the hill
   Of black granite
     Names
       Their bodiless cries

56.

Tree of life with its twelve colored fruits for the seasons
leaves of the tree for the healing of nations
from ground to great wall to the crystal sky
of jasper and sapphire chalcedony emerald
sardonyx and sardius jacinth topaz
chrysoprase amethyst chrysolite beryl
with pearl pearl to circle them all
and no more night nor devil nor death
O prophet come quickly O Lord
Alpha Omega your river your throne of the Lamb
of Light Light Light

57.

sparrows sing differently this morning
they shout their notes
over tame beasts fleeing the fields
of men with bullhorns on their heads
whose bodies are aimed at their brothers
whose mouths are tin trumpets
whose rattlesnakefingers issue their tambourines

turn to us o fathers
who showed us this land to dream by
lift the ceremonial crust from your lips
let the dark stars of your eyes burst the ground

turn to us o mothers
plunge your knifecries into ears
of executioners
strike their hands plucking life from your wombs
stand with us now and in the hour
of resurrections
from disobedient tombs

sanctuary of the possible
sanctuary of the possible
you persist

o imagined country

II. CROSS-COUNTRY JOURNAL

The United States themselves are essentially
the greatest poem.

— WALT WHITMAN, Preface to the First Edition,
Leaves of Grass, 1855

———◆———

With ever watchful eyes and bearing scars, visible and
invisible, I headed North, full of a hazy notion that life could
be lived with dignity, that the personalities of others should
not be violated, that men should be able to confront other
men without fear or shame, and that if men were lucky in
their living on earth they might win some redeeming meaning
for their having struggled and
suffered here beneath the stars.

— RICHARD WRIGHT, *Black Boy*

For Gregory

You took me to Barbara, artist
dying in Chicago at twenty-eight
into primary brightness, she who could
decorate the skull of mortality. You took me
to Lynn in San Diego and Mac on a farm
and drove us where we needed to go,
for this poem. We shared joy
of Mickey Mouse, awe in terrains
of renegade weather,

and for your instruction (the camera),
the explorations of thought,
I thank you, dear Son.

Visit

These hands, the veins tracking them,
these hands in my lap, holding a pen
or a knife and fork, or your hand,
these hands I take journeying
gesture only a passing
motion of the mind, impermanent as the train
that carries them
with my papers and thoughts
and the wonder of views and listening
like an open suitcase
crammed with consciousness
to be worn down with the wheels of this train
toward steel that, too, will move apart
until gathered into an earth
of spirit and substance.

These hands tell me
I must embrace you as I would
embrace the day that gives me
chance after chance, like
different cities
to be born in.

Toward Detroit

Leaping into sight: roads, roadsigns, cars, billboards,
portentous birds—eagle, barnswallow, phoebe,
mourning dove.

The train waits: for water,
for a crossing train,
for wires of cooling heat,
of light.   O
the train,
the train waits.

In the sky: a star,
with us.   A star that moves
as we move.

Dearborn: The Ford Museum

Greenfield Village,
the moon and the sun up ahead.

In the Hall of Technology:
Ford Model B
Ford Models R, S, and
T, "An American Legend"
V-8 Cabriolet
V-8 with all-steel body
Pace Car, Thunderbird . . .

Near the woman in muslin
who makes candles
in candle molds:
The Kearsarge,
a horse-drawn coach
(its run from Maine to New Hampshire),
gypsy wagon, band wagon, calliope
(whose music produced was "loud, harsh, and startling"),
popcorn wagon, stage wagon, omnibus, hansom cab,
speeding cutter, barouche, and runabout,
a 1921 streetcar ("Please have exact fare ready"),
General Tom Thumb's brougham,
chaise, road wagon, buggy, Albany cutter, carryall,
hearse, ornately embellished,
Portland sleigh and Conestoga wagon,
the Pung Sleigh which may have carried
George Washington to church,
travois, craft of American Indian,
and a 1797 coach invoke
wheelwright and blacksmith
the clamor of lost artisans
in their pride.

And the engines.
Hand-pump fire engines once filled
by bucket brigades. The Eagle,
decorated with a framed canvas painting
of a fire fighter and beneath it
a carved eagle. The awesome black locomotive
Lima Allegheny (1941) that traveled 407,008 miles,
its 600 tons equipped with an 8,000 horsepower boiler,
Admiral Byrd's Arctic Expeditionary planes. Engines.
Horses transformed to horsepower.
Engines poised to ride phantoms
in a hall of silent noise.

At Livonia

In the Fisher Body soft trim plant
machines cut and stitch
a new language. From button area
to thermex presses
to numerical magnetic control cutting
and embossing with dielectrics
to overhead conveyors driven by monorail
workers crimp on the hang-on auto panels
send them through stitching
and rubber whiskers
and waterproofing.

In the cutting room:
cookie boards and steel wool dyes.

Through the plant,
riding trams, towmotors, high-lows,
workers guide sail panels
by metal arms
into storage towers.

The sewing: complex,
continuous, mechanical,
with tackdown, design sewing,
chain-lock stitching, join sewing, facings.

In the Fisher Body soft trim plant
everything moves
toward paypoint.

Toward Chicago

Friends on a raft
wheel a small lake around them.

Wave after wave of small towns
laps at the train, the tracks
and a low sun pressing to

Niles, Michigan: your name below
a river of sky.

Trees rest in wake of
dread wind.

Westward

Mass of trees in slow distance
recedes.
Fluttering wheat
streaks the window.

Horses
and cows in a circle
settle
the noon sun.

This is Wisconsin.

Dog on a porch.
Car in a field.
Barley gold and summer swathes
against blue Baraboo Hills.
Families of blue
line the cloud miles
of our eyes.

Lens cannot
stretch enough
and heart cannot
but the joyous mind
approaches.

Toward Montana

Farm woman, alone:
barn, house, and silo
behind you, the mountains
around you, the summer fresh field . . .

On the train slipping past you
my spirit also draws
to the big sky

Companion Poets

I with my suitcase   traveling
these miles ahead   cross-country
with interview tapes   take them
westward   to plant in the park
of the glacier   black blossoms

Nearing Glacier

Past Havre, past Butte, Montana
earth upon earth arises till
clouds are the range.

God in the mountains
indifferent to personal crises
talks eternity
to the clouds.

GLACIER PARK

Impression

And the mind—mind has mountains.
    — GERARD MANLEY HOPKINS

The mountains are there, are not you.
They supplement frail distances, assail
        ego heights. Not you
shooting out of the orange sky
to flame the lakes and matterhorns.
Not you the entombing glacier
paced thirty-six feet a year.
And yet—
                Indian paintbrush
                mountain laurel
                white heather
                glacier lily.

Among Glaciers

Standing we hold tightly the steel handrails. Chief Two-Gun,
the jammer of Swiftcurrent Lake (cut out of Precambrian rock),
takes breeze and height along the shore of St. Mary (three
hundred feet deep), to Lake McDonald on Going-to-the-Sun
Road. Grinnell Glacier is "dirty" with volcanic ash from Mount
St. Helens. We enter the Blackfoot Indian Reservation. Across
Two Medicine Creek through gap between mountains: direct
route to God, to the gods.

Blue blue blue—behind the firs behind the pines
a yellow bus curves the narrow road.

Blue ranges
a density withdrawn
within blue
outside
words.

Grinnell—Alta
between you: glacier.

Firs at lake rim.
Beneath red striations—
time.

impulse to paint the scene

    a brush
       poised at canvas
          is the points possible
             to join the unbreaking
         blue blue blue
       arch of light
     peaks tipped
  at horizon

Logan Pass

At Logan Pass
the Continental Divide
feeds water east and west
through Alpine buttercup
and bear grass. White heather,
lanceleaf spring beauty, red monkeyflower,
mountain laurel, painted cup—
scarlet, white, yellow, orange, pink,
lambstongue, glacier lily . . .

Needlelikeleaves of
red mountain heath hold water
by small surfaces.

Launch Cruise: Lake McDonald

Linda, the forest ranger from
Juneau, Alaska, narrates
our tour, points out
the western red cedar,
the western hemlock, alerts
to white-tailed deer at dusk
and caribou moose. *Pine beetle*
is killing the pine trees. Note
an extension of Pacific rain forest.

Lake McDonald: Rowboat

Clouds among mountains convoke,
threaten wind gust, shower, squall.

Trees at their height, bend. Take
the hour, the swift minute
as a gift. Sunlight *now.*
The moon when it appears. The grass
in season. Up there: moraine,
glacier, waiting.

The grizzly will come down.
The black bear.
The mountain goat sighting
gulls and goshawks.

Suddenly rain.
Row fast. Make
decisions, try
to survive them.

At the lodge, sheltered from rain, we listen to impromptu fiddle, banjo, and guitar. Stephen, Paul, and Gary play "Little Rabbit," thrum, "Some day I'm gonna see her." It rains hard. They play "Campbell's Farewell to Red Gap," "The Red-Haired Boy," and "Black Hills." Rain stops. They promise that life will go well "If you like a ukelele lady, and ukelele lady like-a you."

Mountain Light

Window
overlooking daisies
at lake edge
catches headlights
like fireflies
in the cedars.

Across water
green with glacier milk:

The range. Cannon Mountain.
Lateral moraines.

West Glacier

Last night the sky came down to the mountain
and we huddled in our room in awe.
Whitecaps on the lake took the clouds
and the wind's wintry vibrato
blew a thin note through
the weatherstripping
like a woodwind's reed.

I love the clouds, the clouds that pass, the marvellous clouds.

— CHARLES BAUDELAIRE, "The Stranger"

The clouds   the marvelous clouds
impaled   in this eye
strange sauntering beasts   at prayer
permeate terraces   of stairs to them
then turn   grotesque

building roofs   invite the pressure
of nuances   *les nuages*

A dirt road   between brick and fences
redeems nothing   but footsteps
is bridge or catalyst   is not itself
the thing one seeks   though the passage   be all

Last Day

Behind our cabin
cloud lay on the mountain
like a gray loaf
that thunder waits
to cut.

Toward Seattle

Mount Hood turns
abruptly white
a throat
carving itself clear
of a secret rasp
whispering
to Mount St. Helens:

*My sister, explode
your power.*

Salmon: The Seattle Aquarium

Salmon have one love.
Sometimes swimming
fifteen hundred miles they
return to hail the Columbia River
give birth in their first waters
do the thing for which
they were crafted. Salmon
are watched timewise
in the Aquarium. Spawned
they swim overhead
in a circular
tank. Are freed
by steps
to the sea.

In Transit: Seattle to San Francisco

Somewhere I have traveled
where the mind blows free
among skies   inset   precisely
blue   and the tilled fields
arrayed with poles and wires
designate   this flatness
brown and green   irrigated
Long Island familiar except
this is California

    . . .

I eat/ate breakfast
somewhere east/west
on a train to San Francisco

    . . .

Seattle weather
is bad this year.
Space Needle pricks
fog overflowing
the disk of revolving lunchers
munching clouds and salmon
that swam straight up.

    . . .

Glimpses:

>   Joseph's Fishing Resort
>   Rodeo Bait Shop
>   mudflats at low tide
>   House of Chicken and Submarine
>   Entire World Automotive Center

Gregory says:

>   Take Lex-Lax to relieve
>   writer's block

CALIFORNIA SUITE

Jesus People and Local Two

In Union Square, San Francisco,
on a Saturday, at noon,
Jesus is Lord, they are singing,
palms upward to receive the sun.
Outside the Saint Francis Hotel
Local Two whistles and chants
its picket signs.

The Jesus people protest:
Some want more for less,
want something for nothing.
Industry that shares
is blessed, but you'd better
take care of your spirit.
Pray, don't picket.
Move the hearts
of the people.   Smile.

Meanwhile,
Mount St. Helens
rumbles
and the Congress declares
draft registration.

In Golden Gate Park:
winged unicorn salutes the

sandstone lion dog bird whose
square head frames long teeth.

You wear a stylized beard
O fierce beauty!

Muir Woods

Competition for light is endless.
Smaller trees survive
where great redwood canopy
breaks.   Tenacious
laurel and myrtle
creep into
open spaces.
Branches grope
toward light,
become trunks.

Cover

Each level of branch protects
the level below   one waits for the next
to cover more   I too would grow
heartshaped

Where leaves touch I hear them
like softest bell like pistil at petal
my skin   receives

San Francisco: Point Reyes

for Dana

Fog mists us, collides with
fine rain and raised voices
of hotel workers chanting grievances
while we three gather to reunite
our years in separate cities.

Does childhood leave
a scrimshaw in the spirit?
I whisper your name.

Brother, biologist
insists on Point Reyes.
You drive the rented car.
He sits beside you with maps.
We cross the Golden Gate Bridge
without sunshine.   The road
to Muir Woods
turns narrow.
A fallen car below—
junk monument to the ravine.

Steady, sanguine,
unmindful of climb into fog
and the mountain, you drive
through San Andreas Fault
past cliffs and vultures.

We reach
egrets along the marshes
toward a last, graveled road
sloping outward, a promontory

of improbable flowers
their pink red purple
embedded in rocks above the spray
the sea rising white and bluegreen
like whales sending the long surf
in spouts continuously rolling.

Watch
for cormorant
common murre
oyster catcher
black scoter
peregrine falcon
pelagics at home
in Point Reyes.

You and Gregory
descend pyramidal steps
high as a thirty-story building
to the lighthouse,
climb back
through cold haze grazing the rocks.
At the wind-capped station
you rest, link arms
like years.

I snap your picture,
the lighthouse behind you.

Bird of paradise flower
presses its flame crest
westward through redwoods
their cathedral groves
star pine and liquid amber
night-blooming jasmine
and jade plants

Olive trees are umbrellas
oranges are lanterns in the sun

Beyond this generous house of resonant rooms,
of stucco whiter than snow, the wings
that bear a panoramic essence, deserts remove
to their bleak browns and grays
and solemn cacti, an insolent blooming
against unfallen rain

Live oak, scrub oak, sycamore
lean westward to accept the Orient
reaching its bamboo and palm
through eastward waves
toward oleander mountains
where a century plant, ascending
makes time out of new shoots

Westward—as the East Coast moves
to receive the European style

I learned that each direction one may take
reciprocates
with what is near,
that separate spans of grain and desert
become the binding floor

Cable of a cable car
pulls us uphill   can break
a cord gathers us—
we tie our minutes to it

Lunch in San Diego

Palm trees embrace hibiscus at the beach.
Surf rolls in respectfully before
the Hotel del Coronado, a landmark
(largest wooden building in the country)
with Queen Anne/Victorian cone towers
buffered by pool and outdoor tennis courts.
Competitors entertain us as we watch
the distant yachts lurch past our pleasant lunch
and starlings patrol pastrami and avocados.

Later, on the sand, a man shows me
a bag of seashells that he firmly claims
are valuable. He shares his confidence
that ocean water benefits his foot.
He shows me wounds from World War II:
his ankle scars and those along his rib.
He will continue gathering more shells.

Toward Indiana

Mattress by track recalls
sofa and two armchairs I once saw
outside Delaware, discarded
sociables,

and the signalman flaring ahead
summons the Lighthouse of Asheville
where a retired man signals
the last car of every train:
horizontal arc if o.k.,
vertical if wheels
are on fire.

INDIANA FARM SUITE

connect

apartment buildings
stand like cornstalks
rooted in slaughter
wild hog eyes
blind calves
and screeching
chickens
awire

Modern Milk

Music flows in the cow barn. Farmer
milks sixty-four cows twice a day
with four machines. On clean udders
coated with antiseptic, he places
suction cups. The cows know
his touch, though some may kick,
need clamps from back to groin.

From six a.m. till eight p.m.
milk farmer works. Took no days
off last year, this year, takes two.
Milk farmer prides in labor
and his cows.

Re Clark X (X meaning no horns)

Every breeder interested in raising modern beef-type shorthorns should store a half-dozen canes of Clark semen in reserve. Polled and double registered. Has weighed 3,035. Stands almost 6 feet at the shoulders. Why raise the other kind?

Farm Equipment

At the Aroma Feed Mill:
Charmglow insect killer
electrocutes flies.

In boxes: weevil killer
grain conditioner
Sweetlik molasses mineral lick.

Holdem fencer—110 volts.

Farm boy shows us
hay baler
combine
demonstrates
the bobcat.   Tractor
John Deere 401.0 Diesel
from Blue Mound, Illinois
can split wood.

A honey wagon carts
liquid manure
from the hogs.

In the Automated Chicken House

50,000 screaming chickens
cooped for thirteen months
in groups of five, stuffed into
wire cages so tight
they can hardly
turn around
light on all day
to speed the eggs to
conveyor belts
and boxes.
          Dead chickens
in corners. Could not
take the heat.

Small Farm: Hogs and Chickens

You can't escape
the hogs. Their smell
farms your clothes
licks your lips.
Hogs cool themselves
in mud. They wallow.

Across the yard:
a chicken house.
Rooster struts
in the grass.
Hens hide
among bushes.
These chickens
grow large
in the sun.
They know
what it is
to be a chicken.

Mac

" . . . *the definition of an American.*"
— G. M.V.

In Elegia Sexta, John Milton commends
that the poet of heroic deeds and figures
"live a simple, frugal life, after the fashion
of the teacher who came from Samos," that he drink
pellucid water in a tiny cup of beechen wood,
drink only sober draughts from a pure spring.

You drink spring water,
farmer of grain, polled shorthorns,
rare apples (Spitzenburg, Benoni, the red
June apple of early settlers in Virginia,
the Blue Pearmain you carried from
North Carolina, the Sheepnose).

Your kitchen, Omega, Indiana, end
of a journey cross-country.
At the homemade table, I sit
drawing your face, trying to pen
its weather and wisdom. How to catch
your eyes' punctuation of stories?
Eyes that opened in Gosport and mirror
part-Indian mother; reflect the late
Indiana wife, stepchildren, grandchildren.
What bin or slotted corncrib can hold
your store of tales and qualities?

Breakfast.
Tall in overalls, you bend
to the oven's fresh bread, then mix

125

sausage meat.   You speak of hunting
and mending things, how you
made a violin, climbed
water towers, repaired
flagpoles, worked
as a lineman,
in construction, lived
in Montana, Mississippi,
Georgia, Alabama.

A neighbor calls you
to fix her barn roof.
You like Celtic culture,
went to Britain.
You read history, caring
where people come from.

Church.
Friends move down the pew
to accept us.   At home,
your daughter cooks
our company Sunday dinner.
The family gathers.
Noon light spreads over
the table.   You say grace.

A man—from what boyhood?—
joyously capable.

"We didn't buy much of anything.
We made what we needed."

ABOUT THE AUTHOR

D. H. Melhem, daughter of Lebanese immigrants (with some Greek ancestry) was born in Brooklyn. Having written since the age of eight, she was graduated from high school as "class poet" and read an early poem about the United States to assemblies. At New York University she earned a B.A. *cum laude;* years later an M.A. from City College and a Ph.D. from the City University of New York. Manhattan's Upper West Side, where she raised two children, inspired her *Notes on 94th Street* and *Children of the House Afire.* Recipient of national and international prizes for her poetry, her poems have appeared in anthologies and major literary journals.

As a scholar, Melhem's *Gwendolyn Brooks: Poetry and the Heroic Voice* was the first comprehensive study of the poet and earned her nomination for a Woodrow Wilson Fellowship in Women's Studies. It was published by the University Press of Kentucky (1987). Her *Heroism in the New Black Poetry* (UPK, 1990) was undertaken with a National Endowment for the Humanities Fellowship and won an American Book Award in 1991. She has published over fifty essays in books, critical journals, and periodicals. Her *New York Times Magazine* article earned a New York Heart Association Media Award.

Melhem has read and lectured in venues ranging from cafes, bookstores, and college campuses to Town Hall and the Library of Congress. Her novel *Blight* was published in 1995 by Riverrun Press, the same year that *Rest in Love,* her acclaimed elegy for her mother, was reissued by Confrontation Magazine Press. A member of PEN, the Dramatists Guild, the Authors Guild, Pen & Brush, and other professional societies, she serves on the boards of the International Women's Writing Guild, RAWI (Radius of Arab American Writers), the Shelley Society of New York, and is a contributing editor of *Home Planet News. Country,* a collection in progress since 1972, is her fourth book of poetry.

Typeset by Angel Graphics (Wantagh, NY). Printed by Goldie Press (Wantagh, NY). Bound by Frank Papp (Massapequa, NY). Distributed by Baker & Taylor Books.